AMERICAN PRESIDENTS

GEORGE H.W. BUSH

INDIA JAMES

NORWOOD HOUSE PRESS

Cataloging-in-Publication Data

Names: James, India.
Title: George H. W. Bush / India James.
Description: Buffalo, NY : Norwood House Press, 2027. | Series: American presidents | Includes glossary and index.
Identifiers: ISBN 9781978579842 (pbk.) | ISBN 9781978579859 (library bound) | ISBN 9781978579866 (ebook)
Subjects: LCSH: Bush, George, 1924-2018--Juvenile literature. | Presidents--United States--Biography--Juvenile literature. | Legislators--United States--Biography--Juvenile literature.
Classification: LCC E882.J36 2027 | DDC 973.928092--dc23

Published in 2027 by
Norwood House Press
2544 Clinton Street
Buffalo, NY 14224

Designer: Rhea Magaro
Editor: Kim Thompson

Photo credits: Cover, p. 1, 11 The White House; p. 5 (c) Vividimpressions/Dreamstime.com; pp. 6, 10, 12, 13, 19 Library of Congress; pp. 7, 14 Wikipedia; p. 9 ozer ozyon/Shutterstock.com; p. 15 Bush Library; p. 16 DimaBerlin/Shutterstock.com; p. 17 Krakenimages.com/Shutterstock.com; p. 18 Paul Dempsey/Shutterstock.com; p. 21 Dana Barciniak, U.S. House Office of Photography;

Printed in the United States of America

CPSIA compliance information: Batch #CSNHP27: For further information contact Norwood House Press at 1-800-237-9932.

TABLE OF CONTENTS

Early Years

George Herbert Walker Bush was born on June 12, 1924, in Milton, Massachusetts. He had three brothers and a sister.

George's family moved to Greenwich, Connecticut. He went to school there and at Phillips Academy in Andover, Massachusetts.

Phillips Academy

After George graduated from high school, he **enlisted** in the United States Naval Reserve. He became the youngest pilot to ever serve in the Navy.

George served during World War II. His plane was shot down. George survived. He was awarded a medal for bravery.

Building a Career

After the war, George married Barbara Pierce. He graduated from Yale University.

George started businesses related to oil and gasoline. In 1959, he moved his family to Houston, Texas. That area of the country has many oil businesses.

D-501 C
PROPİLEN

George became a **politician**. He was elected to the **House of Representatives** to represent people from Texas. Then, he was appointed **ambassador** to the **United Nations**. He also represented the U.S. in China.

In 1980, George was elected vice president of the United States. He served two **terms** under President Ronald Reagan.

Presidency

George decided to run for president himself. He was elected as the 41st president of the United States in 1988.

As president, George improved the relationship between the U.S. and the Soviet Union. He helped end the **Cold War**.

The **Gulf War** with Iraq was fought in 1990 and 1991. George led the U.S. to victory.

George cared about Americans. He tried to make their lives better. He signed laws that made companies stop polluting the environment.

He expanded the preschool program Head Start. His interest in schooling made people call him "the education president."

Later Life

After he left the White House, George and Barbara moved back to Houston. George wrote two books. He raised money for people who were hurt by natural disasters.

George loved his family. He and Barbara had six children. Their son Jeb Bush became the governor of Florida. Their son George W. Bush became the governor of Texas. Later, he was elected as the 43rd U.S. president.

George died on November 30, 2018. He is remembered as a president who loved his country. He is remembered for making the world a better place.

Glossary

ambassador (am-BAS-uh-dur): a person sent by a government to represent it in another country or in an organization such as the United Nations

Cold War (kohld wor): the period from 1945 to 1991 when the U.S. and the Soviet Union were in conflict but did not fight an actual war with weapons

enlisted (en-LIS-tid): joined the military

Gulf War (guhlf wor): a conflict in 1990 and 1991 between the country of Iraq and a group of other countries led by the United States

House of Representatives (house uhv rep-ri-ZEN-tuh-tivz): one of the two parts of the United States Congress that is made up of 435 members who help make laws for the country

politician (pah-li-TISH-uhn): a person elected or chosen to hold a government office

terms (turmz): definite or set periods of time; American presidents are elected to a term that lasts four years

United Nations (yoo-NIGH-tid NAY-shuhns): an organization that is made up of 193 nations and that was formed in 1945 to help maintain global peace

Thinking Questions

1. What did George H. W. Bush do during World War II?
2. Where did George and his family move in 1959?
3. For how many terms was George vice president?
4. Why was George known as "the education president"?
5. What is the relationship between President George H. W. Bush and President George W. Bush?

Index

About the Author

India James writes about science, technology, math, and history for young readers. She loves learning new things while writing books. India lives in Ohio with her family.